D1410101

We Use Tools All Day

by Jacqueline A. Ball

illustrations by Ken Bowser

RED CHAIR
·PRESS·

Please visit our website at **www.redchairpress.com** for more
high-quality products for young readers.

About the Author

Jacqueline A. Ball is a Seattle-based writer, editor, and the
former publisher of Scientific American Books for Kids and Weekly
Reader Juvenile Book Clubs. Awards and honors include Booklist
Top 10 Youth Series Nonfiction (ALA), Children's Choice and Parents'
Choice Honors.

Publisher's Cataloging-In-Publication Data
Names: Ball, Jacqueline A. | Bowser, Ken, illustrator.
Title: We use tools all day / by Jacqueline A. Ball ; illustrations by Ken Bowser.

Description: South Egremont, MA : Red Chair Press, [2017] | Series: Space Cat explores STEM
    | Interest age level: 006-009. | Aligned to: Next Generation SCIENCE Standards. | Includes
    glossary, Did You Know sidebars and Try It! feature. | Includes bibliographical references
    and index. | Summary: "People use creative or inventive thinking to adapt the natural
    world to help them meet their needs or wants. All people use tools and technology in their
    life and jobs to solve problems. Space Cat and her pal Dog help readers understand simple
    and complex tools we all use every day."--Provided by publisher.

Identifiers: LCCN 2016954286 | ISBN 978-1-63440-196-8 (library hardcover) |
    ISBN 978-1-63440-200-2 (paperback) | ISBN 978-1-63440-204-0 (ebook)

Subjects: LCSH: Tools--Juvenile literature. | Technology--Juvenile literature. |
    CYAC: Tools. | Technology.

Classification: LCC GN436.8 .B35 2017 (print) | LCC GN436.8 (ebook) | DDC 621.9--dc23

Photo Credits: iStock: 14 Shutterstock, Inc: 4, 5, 6, 7, 8, 9, 10, 11, 12, 13, 14, 15, 16, 17,18,
    19, 20, 21, 22 Cover photo by Jennifer Brown

Space Cat Explores STEM first published by:
Red Chair Press LLC   PO Box 333   South Egremont, MA 01258-0333

Printed in the United States of America
0517 1P CGBF17

Choose the best tool for the job.

Would you eat ice cream with a toothbrush?

Would you brush your teeth with a spoon?

If you did, you wouldn't do a very good job.
You would be using the wrong **tool**.

Tools are helpers. Every tool is specially made to
do a certain job.

If you choose the right tool, you will make the
job easier. If you choose the wrong tool, you
may never finish!

Join Space Cat and her friend Dog to learn about
the tools grownups and kids use all day long.

Look for important new words in **bold** letters.

3

Forks are tools to help us eat solid foods.
Some tools help us drink liquids like water or milk.

Spoons work best for soft foods, like
oatmeal or yogurt. Forks are best for solid
foods like pancakes. The pointy parts,
called tines, dig in to hold food in place.
Forks and spoons have long handles.
The handles keep food away from your
fingers when you carry it to your mouth.

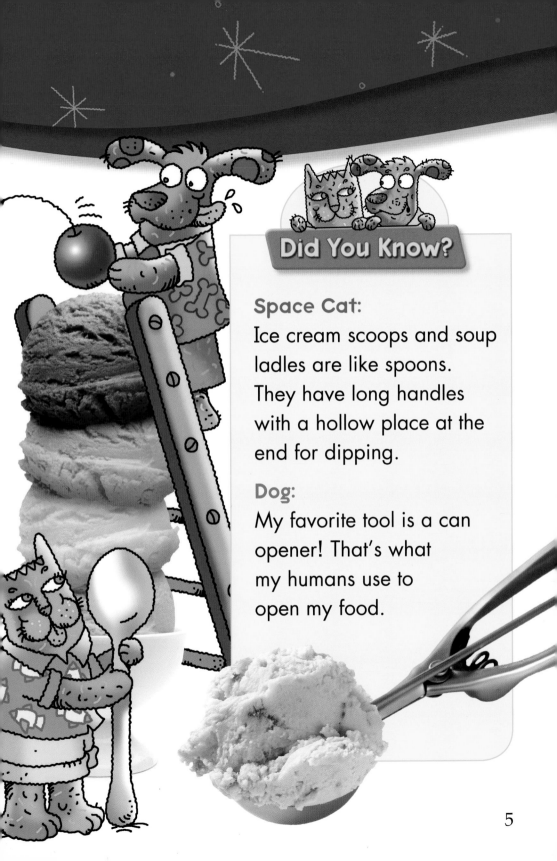

Did You Know?

Space Cat:
Ice cream scoops and soup ladles are like spoons. They have long handles with a hollow place at the end for dipping.

Dog:
My favorite tool is a can opener! That's what my humans use to open my food.

You may use a pencil for schoolwork. Pencil marks rub off with an eraser. You can't erase mistakes when you use a pen. A pencil sharpener will keep pencils pointy and ready too use. Sharp pencils make numbers and letters that are easy for your teacher to read.

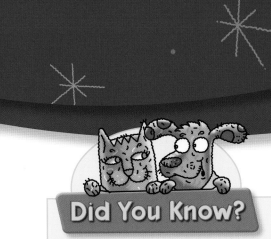

Did You Know?

Space Cat:

A globe is round, like the shape of planet Earth. A map is flat. They are both **geography** tools.

Dog:

Geography tools help us find places and know where we are without sniffing.

What do you like to make at art time?
Choose the best tool.

Crayons have pointed ends to draw shapes and outlines. Markers make thicker lines. Paintbrushes spread lots of color.

Use a glue stick or a stapler to turn your artwork into a book!

Did You Know?

Space Cat:
When you finger paint, your hands are art tools.

Dog:
My paws are art tools when they get muddy. They leave prints everywhere!

9

Books are learning tools. They have stories, pictures, and information.

We get information from the **Internet** on a **computer**. We can also write stories, take tests, or do art on computers with special **software programs**.

Computers and the Internet are learning tools like books. They are part of **technology**. Some people call them tech tools.

Did You Know?

Space Cat:
Big computers stay in one place, like on a table or a desk. That's why we call them desktop computers. Laptops and tablets are small enough to carry around. Smartphones can fit in a pocket.

Dog:
Smartphones do the job of a computer and of a telephone too. That's *really* smart!

Computers and special tools for their job help grownups at work. What tools do you see when you go to the doctor?

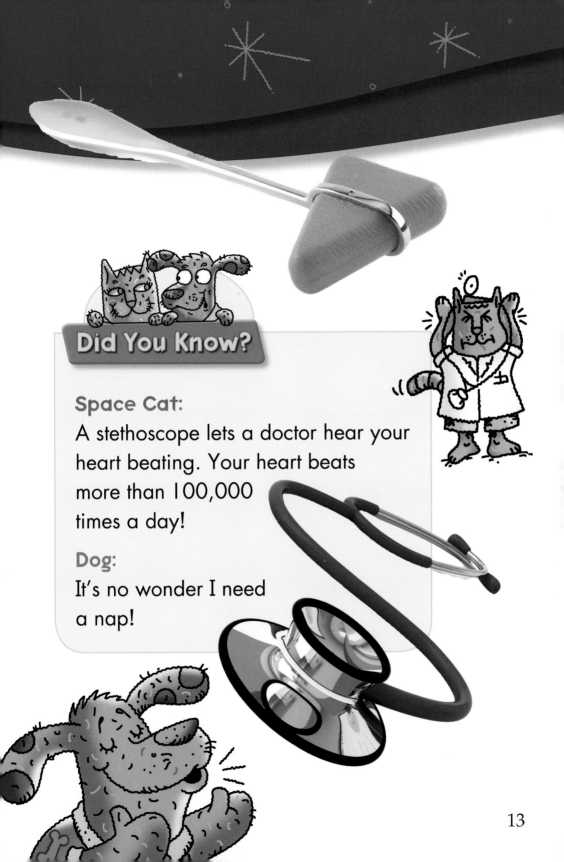

Did You Know?

Space Cat:

A stethoscope lets a doctor hear your heart beating. Your heart beats more than 100,000 times a day!

Dog:

It's no wonder I need a nap!

13

Engineers and construction workers use computers and special tools too.

Try it!

Space Cat:

Ask grownups you know which tools help them do their jobs.

Draw pictures of some of these tools, or find them in a magazine.

Chimps use twigs to pick up insects from their nests.

Humans invent tools to make their work easier. So do many animals. Some chimps and monkeys use stones to break open nuts. They use pieces of grass to hunt for insects.

Did You Know?

Space Cat:
Scientists have seen dolphins, polar bears, and birds all using tools to get food or to protect themselves.

Dog:
My human brings me food!

After dinner it's fun to watch a show or play a video game. A remote lets us control the TV or game station without touching it.

Try it!

Space Cat:

Remotes make our TVs easier and faster to use. Think of a new tool that would help you do a job at home or school. Make a **sketch** of it.

Dog:

Ask a friend to help with your **design**. You'll have more ideas and more fun when you **collaborate**.

At bedtime you wash your face and hands and dry them with a towel.
You brush your teeth with a toothbrush. The **bristles** spread out to scrub every tooth. Don't forget the floss to clean in between!
Did you do a careful job? Check in the mirror.

Good night!

Did You Know?

Space Cat:
Early humans used twigs to clean their teeth. They chewed one end first to make bristles.

Dog:
Dogs clean their teeth when they chew on a bone. That's a tasty tool!

Glossary

Bristles Stiff hairs or fibers

Collaborate Work with another person or a team on a project

Computer A complex machine that stores and works with information

Design A drawing or sketch to show how to make something

Engineer Person who plans and makes equipment, machines and buildings

Geography The study that teaches about Earth's surface

Internet A giant network that connects computers all over the world

Sketch A simple drawing

Software programs Instructions for a computer to do certain things

Technology Scientific inventions and new ideas that solve problems and make life better for people

Tool An object made to do a certain job

Learn More in the Library

Books

Beaty, Andrea. *Iggy Peck, Architect.* Harry Abrams, 2007.

Beaty, Andrea. *Rosie Revere, Engineer.* Harry Abrams, 2013.

Meshon, Aaron. *Tools Rule.* Atheneum, 2014.

Podesto, Martine. *My Science Notebook: Inventions.* Gareth Stevens Publishing, 2009.

Turner, Tracey; Mills, Andrea; Gifford, Clive. *100 Inventions That Made History.* DK Publishing, 2014.

Web Sites

NASA Kids Club
nasa.gov/audience/forstudents/k-4/index.html

PBS Kids Design Squad
pbskids.org/designsquad/

index